Charter Street Cemetery

STORIES FROM THE WITCH TRIALS AND MORE

Lexi Myers

AMERICA
THROUGH
TIME

To the sun to my moon, the light to my dark, the Enid to my Wednesday, my favorite witch, my little sister. I hope to bring the world half the light that you do.

America Through Time®
An imprint of Sutton Publishing Inc
www.through-time.com

First published 2026

ISBN 978-1-63499-574-0

Typeset in 10pt on 13pt Sabon
Printed and bound in the United States of America

CONTENTS

About the Author

Though she's lived in the South for a decade, Lexi was raised in the Northeast. With a love of all things history and horror, the story of the Salem Witch Trials has always interested her. When visiting Salem, the most meaningful stop for her is always the Witch Trial Memorial next to the cemetery. With a love of photography since she was young, Lexi has combined her love of spooky stories and travel on her Instagram page @octoberallyear_ to share with everyone to enjoy. Through her travels, she shares not only the scary stories but also the history that sometimes gets lost along the way.

1

With Trial Memorial: Facing Their Accusors

Before we explore the stories of those that are buried in the cemetery, it is important to acknowledge those who are not buried here. Just outside the cemetery's eastern entrance is the Salem Witch Trials Memorial. Dedicated in 1992, 300 years after the trials, the memorial holds stone benches for each of the twenty victims. Of these twenty that were executed, only three were given a proper burial, their bodies secreted away in the night by their family members.

The location of the memorial is important because, while the accusers were all given proper burials and headstones, no one knows where the majority of the accused witches' bodies ended up. Their memorial rests here, the stone wall giving way to a fence along the back, giving the victims the chance to forever face their accusers for the injustices done to them.

The benches themselves have the name, date, and manner of execution for each victim carved into them. The trees that are planted in the center are locust trees, the type of trees believed to be used as the gallows. And most poignantly, at the entrance to the memorial are quotes taken from the court transcripts. They are stepped over, often missed, and at some points cut off; this symbolizes their pleas of innocence going ignored, not only by the justice system but by others in the community.

The back of the memorial looks into the cemetery, allowing the victims to face their accusers that were given a proper burial in the cemetery.

This is a view over the memorial's wall into the cemetery. This section is where many of the Hathorne family members are buried. On the corner on the left side of the path is the grave of Judge John Hathorne, known by some as the "hanging judge."

This view is into the cemetery from the memorial at night.

From this part of the cemetery you can see in the memorial.

Each side of the memorial contains ten stone benches, one for each of the victims, with their name, manner of execution, and date of death on them.

The trees that sit in the middle of the memorial are locust trees. The executions are believed to have taken place at Proctor's Ledge, where there is also a memorial to the victims. Locust trees were what would have been used as the gallows.

"I do plead not guilty," Mary Bradbury.

"I can deny it to my dying day," William Hobbs.

"God knows I am innocent," Elizabeth Howe, age fifty-five, July 19, 1692.

At the edges of the memorial, you can see where the words from the victims have been cut off. On the top line you can see the end of William Hobbs' words, "I can deny it to my dying day." Below, you can see the start of, "I am no witch," which was spoken by Bridget Bishop, who died June 10, 1692.

"Oh Lord, help me!" Rebecca Nurse, July 19, 1692.

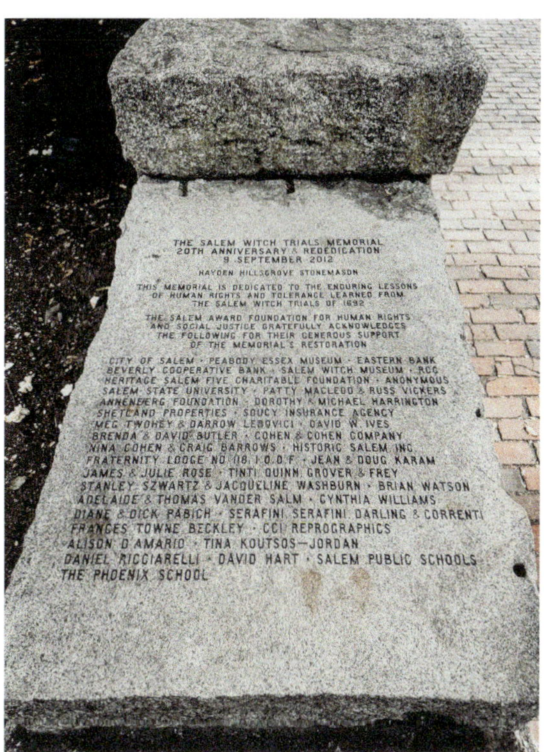

"This memorial is dedicated to the enduring lessons of the human rights and tolerance learned from the Salem Witch Trials of 1692."

While the accusations and arrests began in March of 1692, the executions would begin with Bridget Bishop on June 10.

Bridget was born sometime in the 1640s as she was in her early fifties at the time of her death. She was somewhat of an "easy target" for accusations as she did not live by Puritanical norms. She owned her own land, dressed "provocatively" by wearing lace, and was described as "belligerent and brash." She was married three times, with her second marriage being extremely abusive. She and that husband, Thomas Oliver, often ended up in court over their fights. She was accused, tried, and executed in a few weeks, which was the shortest time frame of any of the victims. Likely not helping her case, her husband, daughter, and son-in-law were not at her trial.

She was the only victim to be hanged alone, dying on June 10, 1692. It is said she "insisted on her innocence even as she climbed the ladder."

Bridget Bishop was the first one tried, convicted, and executed for witchcraft; she was sixty years old.

After Bridget came Sarah Good, Elizabeth Howe, Susannah Martin, Rebecca Nurse, and Sarah Wildes on July 19, 1692.

Sarah Good has descriptions such as, "sullen, combative, unkempt," a "local menace," and "caustic at best, insolent at worst." She often wasn't present at church either, though she explained this as being due to the state of her clothing; the family was poor, and she didn't have anything proper to wear. Like Bridget, these things made her an easier target for accusations. She was homeless, begging in order to survive. This would be hard for anyone, but she was born into a well-off family; the cycle of debt she was in started when her father committed suicide when she was only eighteen. Her first husband died in debt, and her second husband wasn't very successful in providing for them.

Sarah suffered greatly in prison. There are conflicting reports on whether she was pregnant when she went to prison or had just given birth, but in either case, her infant daughter Mercy died in the jail's conditions. She also had to watch her five-year-old daughter, Dorothy, suffer in these conditions as well, as she had also been arrested for witchcraft. Her husband proved to be no help at her examination, stating, "She is an enemy to all good." At the time of her execution she said, "You are a liar. I am no more a witch than you are a wizard."

Elizabeth Howe was in her fifties, a mother of six and wife to a farmer who she cared for after he had gone blind. She was related to another victim, Rebecca Nurse, by marriage. Her husband's brother, John Howe, was married to Sarah Towne. Sarah was the niece of victims Rebecca Nurse, Mary Easty, and Sarah Cloyce, who were all sisters. This family was particularly targeted during the trials.

Susannah Martin was a seventy-one-year-old widow that had been previously accused of witchcraft in 1669. She had been cleared of those charges, but people had a tendency not to forget. Sarah Wildes was another previously accused witch, having been accused back in 1676. Her accusation and subsequent execution showed that no one was safe; she was the mother of a town constable.

Rebecca Nurse was also seventy-one, a great-grandmother, and a long-standing member of the church. She was almost deaf and had been ill in the weeks leading up to her arrest. Part of her accusations stated that the reason she hadn't been going out was because she was recovering after sending her specter to torment the "afflicted" girls. She was still sick when she was arrested, leaving her husband "frustrated and fuming" as he followed them.

Unlike Sarah Good, Rebecca's husband was her biggest supporter. Rebecca had been initially found not guilty, but the jurors were forced to reconsider after fits from the "afflicted." Rebecca, hard of hearing, was unable to answer their questions as she did not hear them. Not only was she nearing deafness, but the courtrooms themselves were nothing short of a circus. When she didn't answer, her silence was taken as guilt. After she was found guilty, her husband, Francis, put together petitions and papers to take to the governor in Boston to get her a reprieve; it worked. However, the "afflicted" fell into further fits upon learning this, causing the governor to withdraw the reprieve. Before her death, Rebecca was excommunicated from the church. So, while she knew her innocence from the charges, she was likely convinced she was going to hell as she was formally kicked out of the church. Rebecca was one of the three victims taken by their families to be given a proper burial.

Sarah Good was pregnant when she, along with her five-year-old daughter, Dorothy, were arrested. She gave birth in prison but lost her daughter, Mercy, due to the conditions of the jail. It was claimed that her infant daughter's spirit accused her mother of murder as well as of being a witch. She died eight days after her thirty-ninth birthday on July 19, 1692. Dorothy remained in prison until December. (Some sources said that Sarah had given birth before going to prison, some after; in either event, baby Mercy was lost in the jail.)

"If it was the last moment I was to live, God knows I am innocent," Elizabeth Howe, age fifty-five, July 19, 1692.

Above left: "I have no hand in witchcraft," Susannah Martin, age seventy, July 19, 1692.

Above right: "It is false. I am clear. For my life now lies in your hands," Rebecca Nurse, age seventy-one, July 19, 1692. She was found not guilty, but after fits from the "afflicted," the judge had jurors reconsider. They eventually found her guilty. Her husband, Francis, gathered a petition and other documents to take to Boston to the governor; Rebecca was then granted a reprieve. The governor soon reversed this though after protests in Salem among the "afflicted."

Right: "I never saw the book in my life and I never saw these persons before," Sarah Wildes, age sixty-five, July 19, 1692. Many of the "afflicted" accused the victims of trying to get them to sign "the devil's book" to sign away their souls.

One of the unique aspects of the Salem witch trials is that, while most trials involve women, this trial also had its share of accused men. August 19 was when the majority of those men would be executed. This day saw the deaths of George Burroughs, George Jacobs, John Proctor, John Willard, and Martha Carrier.

George Burroughs was a minister and graduate of Harvard. He had once served as a minister in Salem but later left to go back to Maine. In an oversimplified version of events, there was dispute over the minister position by different factions that had formed in Salem Village. Burroughs was picked over someone else, leaving those who didn't want him as minister with a bad taste in their mouths, which set him up for failure in the following decade as the accusations and trials rolled around. Not only was he buried in an unmarked grave, but they also stole his clothing and replaced them with a lesser quality set so someone else could have his nice clothing.

George Jacobs and John Proctor were the other two victims who were given a proper burial after their deaths. Jacobs was described as "jaunty, convivial," and that he "had a rollicking sense of humor." In addition to questioning George, they questioned his son, daughter-in-law, and granddaughter. His granddaughter, Margaret, had confessed to practicing witchcraft with her grandfather; she was only twelve years old. He was eighty-three years old when he was executed.

John Proctor is distinguished as the first man to be accused during the trials, arrested shortly after his wife Elizabeth. He became a target as he didn't believe the so-called "afflicted" girls. His son, William, was also questioned but was later found not guilty. John and Elizabeth would not be so lucky. While John's execution was scheduled, Elizabeth's was delayed due to her pregnancy. She gave birth on January 27, 1693, in jail to a son she named John; her execution was scheduled for February 1, but the governor stepped in at this point and gave them all reprieves.

John Willard was a young father, around thirty years old when he was executed. He was a constable in the village who had been making arrests of those accused but eventually refused to continue doing so as things escalated. He tried to run before he could be arrested but was eventually caught. Between refusing the arrests and trying to run before his own, he seems to have sealed his own fate.

Martha Carrier was questioned for witchcraft along with her two sons, Richard and Andrew. Much like Bridget Bishop, she didn't conform to Puritanical norms. She had had a child out of wedlock and had rumors swirling for a while that she was a witch; there were those that even referred to her as "the queen of hell."

At the time of his execution, Reverend George Burroughs perfectly recited the Lord's Prayer, which is something witches were not supposed to be able to do. To explain this away, those in the crowd said that the devil must have been whispering it to him. He was approximately forty-two years old, August 19, 1692.

"I am wronged. It is a shameful thing that you should mind these folks that are out of their wits," Martha Carrier, age about forty-two, August 19, 1692.

"Because I am falsely accused. I never did it," George Jacobs, age eighty-three, August 19, 1692.

Above: "The innocency of our Case with the Enmity of our Accusers and our Judges, and Jury, whom nothing but our Innocent Blood will serve their turn, having Condemned us already before our Tryals, being so much incensed and engaged against us by the Devil, makes us bold to Beg and Implore your Favourable Assistance of this our Humble Petition to his Excellency, That if it be possible our Innocent Blood may be spared, which undoubtedly otherwise will be shed, if the Lord doth not mercifully step in," John Proctor's petition, age sixty, August 19, 1692.

Below left: "Sir, as for sins I am guilty of, if the minister asks me I am ready to confess … Sir, I cannot confess that which I do not know," John Willard, age about thirty-five, August 19, 1692.

Below right: "Now tell us the truth in this matter."

"I hope through the goodness of God I shall, for that matter I never had no hand in, in my life," Giles Corey, age eighty-one, September 19, 1692. Giles refused to enter a plea, so they attempted to force one by pressing him with heavy stones; he eventually died from the torture. His last words were said to be, "More weight."

Giles Corey is the only victim that didn't hang during the witch trials. Instead, he died from "*peine forte et dure.*" After initially testifying against his own wife, Giles was arrested as well. Seeing how the trials were going, he knew that he would likely be found guilty; he believed that, if this happened, the town would seize his land and property. So, when it came time for his trial, he refused to enter a plea. The court's response for this was torture, the "*peine forte et dure*," where he would be crushed slowly under heavier and heavier stones until he entered a plea. He never did, dying instead from the torture. He's the only person in this country's history to die in this manner.

Three days after Giles' death, September 22, was what would be the final round of executions during the trials. This day would see the deaths of Giles' wife, Martha Corey, along with Mary Easty, Alice Parker, Mary Parker, Ann Pudeator, Wilmot Redd, Margaret Scott and Samuel Wardwell.

Like Martha Carrier, Martha Corey previously had a child out of wedlock. She eventually married and had another son; widowed by her first marriage, she married Giles in 1690. After the initial examinations, like some of the other victims, Martha began to disbelieve the "afflicted." She even went as far as to hide Giles' saddle to keep him from attending further examinations. And, like the other victims, this made her a target.

Mary Easty was the younger sister of Rebecca Nurse. Their younger sister Sarah Cloyce was also arrested but was later released. Joanna Towne, their mother, had been accused of witchcraft years prior, and as we've seen with other victims, previous accusations are never forgotten. Mary was fifty-eight and a mother of seven; it's said that nearly everyone present at her execution was brought to tears. Mary's reputation continues to be brought up as recently as 2013 with the release of *The Conjuring*. In the movie there is a scene where they claim that the woman haunting the property, Bathsheba Sherman, was not only a witch but she was descended from Mary Easty, misrepresenting both women.

Alice Parker's medical history is part of what made her a target. She struggled with catalepsy, which is where a person can suffer from stiff limbs, decreased respiration and other slowed bodily functions. Essentially, they can appear as if they are dead. And while catalepsy was a known illness at the time, it was used against her at the time of the trials, with many saying her body was freezing up like that due to her specter leaving her body to attack the "afflicted." Also against her was the fact that she may have been a friend of Bridget Bishop, she had once predicted a friend's husband died at sea, and she had previous run-ins with the family of Mary Warren, one of the girls making accusations. She had once asked Mary's father for help harvesting the grass on her property and he said he would if he had time, which he didn't. They got into an argument over it, and she's reported to have said, "He had better he had done it." Shortly after this, Mary's mother and sister became ill; her mother died, and her sister became deaf.

Mary Parker was in her fifties when she died and had been considered "a respectable member of the community" who had "no previous brushes with the law nor quarrels with neighbors." Like others, your standing in the community did not guarantee your safety; anyone could be targeted at any time.

As with many others, Ann Pudeator's past came back to haunt her. Widowed in 1674, she became a nurse to help support their five children. In 1675, she was caring for Isabel Pudeator; after her death, she married Isabel's husband, Jacob. He was twenty years younger than her, dying in 1682 and leaving her his estate. She may have thought she was safe after her first accusation as she had been examined but then released; unfortunately, she was accused again and this time kept in prison.

Wilmot Redd, much like Bridget Bishop and Sarah Good, did not have the support of her husband during her trial; no one even came to visit her in jail. Described as "cantankerous" and "irritable," there was a rhyme made up about her after she had sold some neighbors sour butter (something she did to help her husband's income):

Old Mammy Redd

Of Marblehead

Sweet milk could turn

To mold in churn.

Margaret Scott's husband, Benjamin, died in 1671. At the time of his death, he left her 67 pounds and 17 shillings (or $87.72). Today, this would equate to roughly $6,967. Margaret lived off that amount of money for twenty years; similar to Sarah Good, she was often begging in order to get by, making her unpopular.

Samuel Wardwell is noted to be the only person to confess to subsequently hang. At the time, it was believed that if you confessed you would not be tried and executed. Because of this, he was a part of the trials, accusing other victims alongside the "afflicted." Once he realized that his confession would not prevent his death, he tried to recant but it was too late. His wife, their daughter, and his stepdaughter were all also accused; the accusations likely rose, in part, due to Samuel's "knack" for predicting who would marry and who would pass away, being described as a "fortune teller." The daughters were found not guilty, but his wife was, though she was never executed.

"I am an innocent person, I never had to do with witchcraft since I was born. I am a gospel woman ... The Lord open the eyes of the magistrates and ministers, the Lord show his power to discover the guilty," Martha Corey, age seventy-three, September 22, 1692.

"I petition to your honours not for my own life, for I know I must die and my appointed time is set but the Lord knows it is, that if it be possible no more innocent blood may be shed which undoubtedly cannot be avoided in the way and course you go in. I question not but your honours does to the utmost of your powers in the discovery and detecting of witchcraft and witches and would not be guilty of innocent blood for the world but by my own innocence I know you are in the wrong way the Lord in his infinite mercy," Mary Easty's petition, age fifty-eight, September 22, 1692.

"I am not guilty ... I know nothing of it ... I never spoke a word to her in my life," Alice Parker, age about sixty, September 22, 1692.

"How long have ye been in the snare of the devil?"

"I know nothing of it. There is another woman of the same name in Andover," Mary Parker, age about fifty-five, September 22, 1692.

"I never saw the devil's book nor knew that he had one," Ann Pudeator, age about seventy-one, September 22, 1692.

"My opinion is they [the afflicted] are in a sad condition," Wilmot Redd, age about fifty-seven, September 22, 1692.

Many of the documents pertaining to the trial of Margaret are missing, so there is no record of her response to the charges. Margaret Scott, age seventy-six, September 22, 1692.

It didn't take long after the trials were over for people to realize their grave mistakes. One of the judges, Samuel Sewall, expressed his guilt in 1697. In 1702, the trials were officially declared "unlawful." In 1711, restitution was paid to the family members of some of the victims, though to quote Mary Easty's husband Isaac, " ... my trouble and sorrow of heart in being deprived of her after such a manner which this world can never make me any compensation for." The families were paid the following amounts, with the amount in parenthesis being the dollar amount today:

Elizabeth Howe: 12£ ($438.39)

George Jacobs: 79£ ($8,116.49)

Mary Easty: 20£ ($2,054.54)

Mary Parker: 8£ ($821.97)

George Burroughs: 50£ ($5,137.53)

Giles & Martha Corey: 21£ ($2,157.78)

Rebecca Nurse: 25£ ($2,568.37)

John Willard: 20£ ($2,054.54)

Sarah Good: 30£ ($3,082.20)

Martha Carrier: 7£ and 6 shillings ($749.70)

Samuel Wardwell: 36£ and 15 shillings ($3,775.52)

John Proctor: 150£ ($15,411.81)

Sarah Wildes: 14£ ($1,438.26)

These victims also had their convictions reversed; Rebecca Nurse and Giles Corey had their excommunications reversed in 1712 as well. Others had their convictions reversed and restitutions paid, but for this book I am solely focusing on the victims that were executed.

At the time of the 1711 Act to Reverse the Attainders of George Burroughs et al. for Witchcraft, family members did not come forward for the following victims: Bridget Bishop, Susannah Martin, Alice Parker, Ann Pudeator, Wilmot Redd and Margaret Scott. Because of this, their convictions were not overturned at this time. Ann's was overturned in 1957, 265 years after the trials. Bridget, Susannah, Alice, Wilmot, and Margaret were finally exonerated on Halloween 2001.

Whenever you are visiting Charter Street Cemetery make sure to pay a visit to the nearby memorial for the witch trial victims. Many were not given a proper burial, their families were not given nearly the restitution they deserved, and several were not exonerated until nearly a decade after the memorial was dedicated. It is endlessly important to acknowledge their suffering and loss after what happened to them.

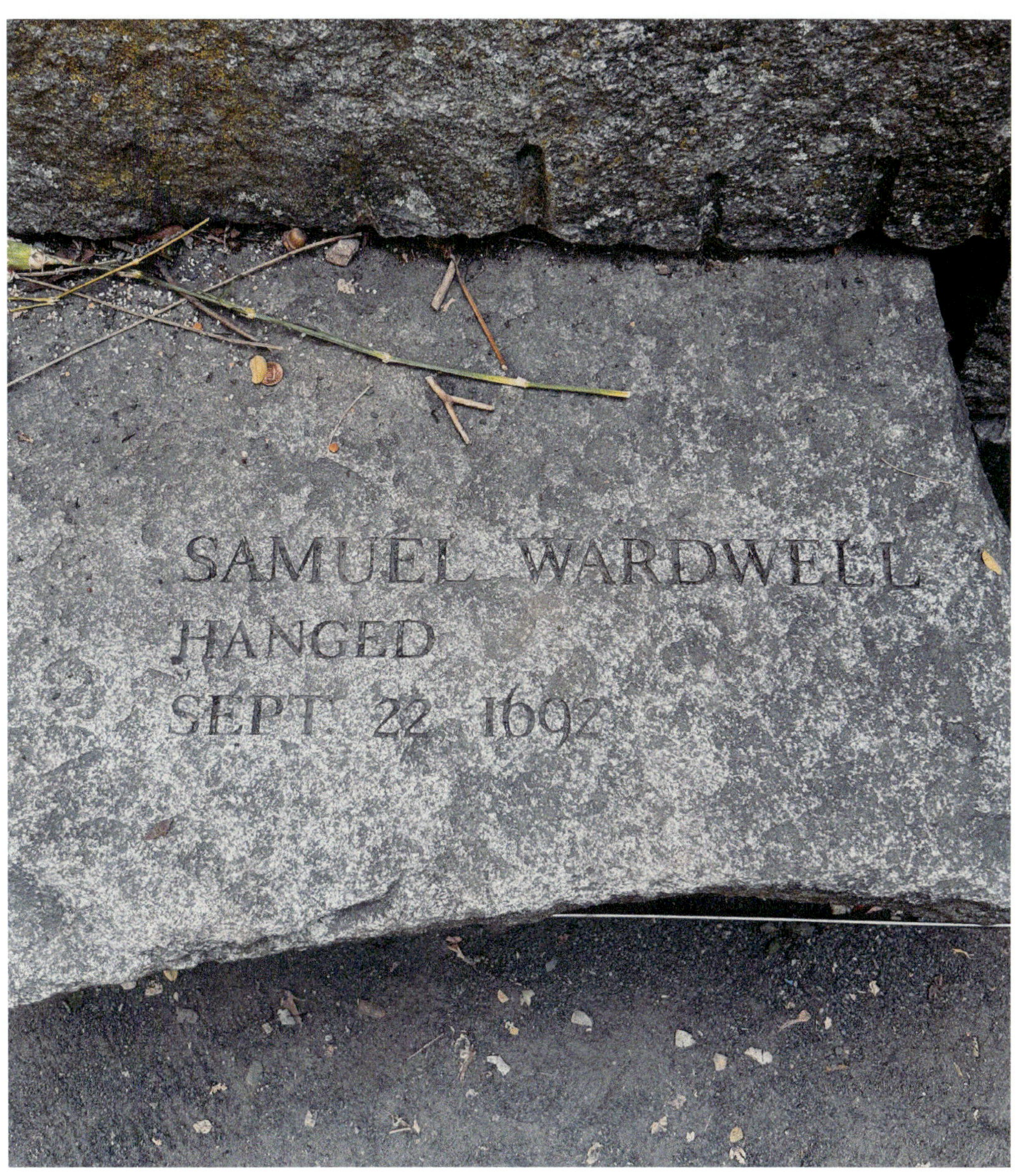

"At execution, while he was speaking to the people, protesting his innocency, the executioner being at the same time smoking tobacco, the smoke coming in his face interrupted his discourse; those accusers said that the devil did hinder him with smoke," Samuel Wardwell, age forty-nine, September 22, 1692.

2

With Trial Connections: Tragedy's Long Reach

Researching this cemetery wasn't difficult because information was scarce; it wasn't. The challenge lay in the story itself. Great tragedy touches everyone in a community, with some becoming victims and others becoming accusers. That is why the memorial stands where it does, so the victims can forever face those who accused them.

I want to be clear: not everyone that will be mentioned in this chapter was directly involved in the witch trials. Some are relatives and descendants that I found connected to the trials; with some families, I imagine it hung over their heads in the years after, especially after the Act in 1711. This chapter is meant to highlight the people that the victims' memorial is meant to be facing, looming over for eternity. Because while some showed remorse, others regretted nothing.

Note: Please be respectful of all cemetery rules when visiting and remember you are visiting the final resting place of many. Every place of burial deserves to be treated with the utmost respect.

John Higginson was one that was more directly part of the witch trials, and his second wife, Margaret, had ties as well. John was born on August 20, 1675, to parents John and Sarah as the oldest son in nine siblings. His father, John Sr., was a minister beginning in 1660. Hannah, his first wife, was born on April 4, 1676, to Samuel and Elizabeth Gardner; she had only one younger brother. They married in Salem on September 11, 1695, and had six children: Elizabeth, John, Samuel, Sarah, Francis and Henry. Sadly, Francis was stillborn and neither Samuel or Henry would live past one year old. Hannah died June 24, 1713, and John remarried Margaret Sewall the following year on November 11, 1714. They had four children together, though only one survived childhood: they had unnamed twins (a boy and girl) in 1715 that died a day after birth, Stephen, who lived to adulthood, and Nathaniel who lived 1718–1719.

If Margaret's maiden name of Sewall sounds familiar, it should. Her father, Stephen, was the younger brother of Samuel Sewall, one of the judges during the witch trials. John's father had been involved in questioning Dorothy Good, the daughter of Sarah Good, who was only five years old.

John was also a part of the witch trials, being sworn as a justice of the peace in June of that year. He was there when Ann Foster was questioned, who ultimately confessed; she named Martha Carrier and George Burroughs in her confessions. Even though John

Sr. and John Jr. were part of the witch trial examinations, that didn't stop accusations from coming into their own family. John Jr.'s older sister, Ann, had been accused of witchcraft. She confessed and was jailed for a time but was ultimately never tried and was returned to the care of her father; she had been living with him after her husband had left her and their children, with many thinking her behavior after this event led to her accusations. Her own father described her as having an "overbearing melancholy" and to be "crazed in her understanding."

Today, the location where John Sr.'s home once sat is home to the Salem Witch Museum.

The grave on the right belongs to John Higginson. To the left is the grave of John's first wife, Hannah. Hannah and John died in 1713 and 1718, respectively. Many are likely familiar with where his father's former home once stood; he lived on and owned the land where the Salem Witch Museum sits today on Salem Common.

This is the grave of Mary Andrew, born Mary Higginson on October 14, 1708. Her father, Nathaniel, and John Higginson were brothers. She married Nathaniel Andrew on September 20, 1729, and they had eight children. She died on October 3, 1747.

These graves belong to Edmond and Martha Batter. Edmond (left) was the only child of Edmond and Mary, born January 8, 1673. He first married Martha on October 26, 1699, and they had ten children, though four died in infancy. Martha died in 1713, and Edmond remarried Barbara Hide on May 25, 1714. She had no children from her previous marriage; they had one son together, but he died in infancy. Barbara died in 1724. Edmund remarried widow Hannah Higginson on September 25 of that year; she was John Higginson's sister-in-law (both he and his brother Nathaniel both married women named Hannah).

A path winds its way through Salem's former residents.

The wall for the memorial can be seen from this portion of the cemetery.

Sally Gardner is a distant relative by marriage to those making accusations during the trials. Born to William and Sarah Fairfield on January 4, 1766, she had one younger sister named Martha. She married Jonathan Putnam Gardner on November 26, 1791, when she was twenty-five. They had two children during their marriage: Jonathan Jr. in 1792 and William in 1794. While William would live into adulthood, Jonathan Jr. died on December 17, 1795, when he was only three. Sally died less than a week later on December 23 from typhus fever.

As with a lot of old cemeteries, there is more information available about Sally's husband than there is about her. He was a merchant with a warehouse on Union Wharf, selling things from hemp to sail cloth to sugar. During the American Revolution he commanded a privateer named the *Union*. His looks are even described, with him standing five feet five inches with a "brown" complexion. After Sally's death, he remarried Lucia Dodge; they never had children and when he died intestate, everything went to his son William. Those interested in where his home once stood can find it to be where the Essex Institute stands today.

Jonathan's middle name, Putnam, is what caught my eye in relation to the witch trials. The Putnam family were some of the primary accusers and witnesses during the trials. Jonathan's mother, Sarah, was a Putnam family member. Her great-grandparents were John and Rebecca Putnam. When George Burroughs came to Salem initially, he stayed with the Putnams for a time while the parsonage was being built. Incidents that occurred around the home, such as allegedly telling his wife to "keep his secrets," were used against him later at trial. John's grand-niece was Ann Putnam, one of the "afflicted" girls making the accusations.

The following was taken from Sally Gardner's obituary in the Salem Gazette: "She was a woman of native worth, and of the most useful accomplishments. She possessed a cheerful temper, but her manners were always without offense. Her readiness of thought from her tenderness of mind, was incapable of exciting disgust, or doing an injury. From her natural disposition, her charity was equal, and constant. Her affability was directed by an uninterrupted flow of affection, towards all who approached her... She has left the husband she loved, and one child, and can never be left from the memory of her friends, who love the virtues she possessed. Her aged mother demands our most sincere condolence."

This row of graves shows several Gardner family members. The grave to the left is Lucia Gardner, Jonathan's second wife after Sally's death. The grave to the far right is her father-in-law, Jonathan Gardner Sr. The broken grave at the center belongs to Hannah Gardner, Jonathan Sr.'s younger sister.

Many graves rest in the shade of this tree.

The Hathorne family has both literary and witch trial connections. It all starts with Judge John Hathorne, born August 4, 1641, to parents William and Ann. His father had been a judge as well, coming to the colonies on the ship *Arabella* in 1630. John married Ruth Gardner on March 22, 1674; he was thirty-two and she was less than half his age at fourteen. While they were married, they had seven children: John, Nathaniel, Ruth, Ebenezer, William, Joseph, and Ruth. Their first daughter Ruth died in 1694; their second daughter was born that same year, so they gave her her sister's name. All their sons would go on to become sea captains.

John was the chief examiner during the witch trials, always assuming guilt as he questioned the accused. He seems to have gotten this trait from his father who was known as a "bitter persecutor" of Quakers. A clear conflict of interest by today's standards, he was given some of the Wardwell land after Samuel was executed, so he profited from the deaths. And, unlike Samuel Sewall, he didn't show any remorse after the fact. He went on to be appointed to superior court in 1702 and died in 1717.

His son Joseph was born the year of the witch trials. He married Sarah Bowditch, and they had eight children: William, Joseph, John, Sarah, Ebenezer, Nathaniel, Daniel, and Ruth. William was born on February 20, 1715. He married Mary Touzel on March 29, 1741, and they had twelve children together; William died in 1794 and Mary in 1805. Mary's older sister, Susannah, married William's younger brother John. The Touzel sisters present another tie to the witch trials for the Hathorne family.

Susannah and Mary were the granddaughters of Philip and Mary English, a wealthy couple accused and arrested during the witch trials. Thankfully, they managed to escape prison and Massachusetts for a time until the trials ended. When they came back though, their lives were never the same as Mary's health declined and much of Philip's assets had been seized; Philip brought a lawsuit against the sheriff at the time, George Corwin. The story goes that after Sheriff Corwin died, Philip stole the body and held it for ransom, with the Corwin family giving him their family silver as payment for the body.

John Hathorne was born on May 22, 1719 (or 1720 depending on the family tree). He and Susannah married on October 16, 1746, and they had twin children in 1749, Susannah and John. Their daughter Susannah was noted as living in the Turner Mansion, aka the House of the Seven Gables. Susannah was also said to be in possession of the silver her grandfather ransomed from the Corwin family, but it's hard to tell if this is accurate or just a family story as records of these events don't exist.

Daniel Hathorne was born on August 22, 1731, as the seventh of Joseph and Sarah's eight children. He married Rachel Phelps on October 21, 1756, and their home still stands today at 27 Union Street. They were married until his death in 1796, and they had ten children: Daniel, William, Rachel, Sarah, Eunice, John, Judith, Nathaniel, Ruth, and Rachel. Daniel served during the American Revolution and there was even a song written about him.

Bold Hawthorne was commander,
A man of real worth,
Old England's cruel tyranny
Induced him to go forth.

Their son Nathaniel would go on to marry Elizabeth Manning; their oldest son, Nathaniel Jr., is the famous author of *The Scarlet Letter*, *The House of the Seven Gables*, and many other works. The story goes that he started to go by Hawthorne with a *W* added to it to distance himself from his family's history.

The headstone of Judge Hathorne of the witch trials was encased in cement and then granite in order to preserve it. His home once stood at 114 Washington Street, which is ironically where the *Bewitched* statue sits today.

This is the grave of William Hathorne who died April 4, 1794, when he was seventy-nine years old, though his grave notes him as being eighty.

This is the grave of Mary Hathorne, one of the granddaughters of Philip and Mary English that married into the Hathorne family. She married William, one of the grandsons of Judge Hathorne, on March 29, 1741. During their marriage they would have twelve children.

This photo shows witch trial judge John Hathorne buried next to his grandson William, one of his two grandsons that married a granddaughter of a witch trial victim.

"Here lie interr'd the remains of Mr. John Hathorne, son of Capt. Joseph Hathorne & Grandson to the Honourable John Hathorne, Obt. Febr. 6th 1750: Aetatis 28." His headstone notes that he was twenty-eight, but if he was born in 1719 or 1720 like the family trees indicate, he would have been thirty or thirty-one. Record keeping was much different than it is today, so it's hard to say which is the accurate date/age.

At the center of this photo is the grave of Captain Daniel Hathorne; to his left is his wife, Rachel.

This photo shows the graves of brothers John and Daniel Hathorne; at the center is the grave of Judith Archer, one of Daniel's granddaughters. Judith was the daughter of Daniel's daughter, Judith, and her husband, George.

This photo focuses on the grave of little Judith Archer. Born on July 3, 1796, she died on March 13, 1801, from scarlet fever when she was only four.

Deliverance Parkman was a merchant who was married four times. Born in Boston to Elias and Bridget in 1651, he was baptized on August 10 of that year. He first married Sarah Veren in 1673, and they had five children: Deliverance, Sarah, Veren, Abigail, and Dorcas. It's likely Abigail and Dorcas didn't survive childhood or may have been stillborn as they appear on family trees but without any dates. His wife Sarah died in November 1681, and their son Deliverance died that same year.

There is no exact date for when he married Mehitable Waite, it's just noted as being "after January 14, 1682." They had a daughter, Mehitable, in 1683; in December 1684, Deliverance was widowed again. He married again on June 3, 1685, to Margaret Gardner. They had three children: Deliverance Jr., Samuel, and Margaret. Deliverance died in 1688 when he was two and Samuel died the same year when he was one. Margaret died the following year in March 1689.

Deliverance married for the fourth time later that year. He married Susannah Gedney, widow of John Gedney. She had two adult children when they married, sons William and Nathaniel. Deliverance's surviving children from his first three marriages were Sarah (11), Veren (8), Mehitable (6), and Margaret (1). Deliverance and Susannah would not have children together. Susannah's first husband, William and Nathaniel's father, was the older brother of Bartholomew Gedney who was a magistrate during the witch trials. Susannah and Bartholomew co-owned a tavern known as "Widow Gedney's" where they served those attending the trials.

The Wainwright family, like Sally Gardner, is related to the witch trials through marriage. They, however, are related to one of the victims. Francis Wainwright was born in England in 1616, coming to America in 1630 as an apprentice. He and his wife, Philippa, married in 1648. They had eight children together: John, Sarah, Mary, Martha, Simon, Mehitable, Francis Jr., Benjamin, and Elizabeth. Their daughter, Martha, married Joseph Proctor around 1660. Joseph was the younger brother of John Proctor.

The last family tie to the witch trials that I will be sharing relates to the grave of William Jr. and Elianor Hollingworth. William Sr. and Elianor were married in Salem in 1654. Family trees differ on how many children they had, but the two that I'll be focusing on are William Jr. and Mary. William Sr. was lost at sea in 1677. In 1688, William Jr. died, and it's noted on the grave he was thirty-three years old. Elianor died the following year in 1689 when she was fifty-nine. William Jr. and Elianor were buried here by Mary who, by this time, was now Mary English. She and her husband Philip were among the accused in the witch trials, though they thankfully survived.

These are the graves of Margaret Parkman (left) & Deliverance Parkman (right). They were married in Marblehead in 1685. Margaret would die four years later.

Hannah Gedney (left) and William Gedney (right) were wed on May 7, 1690, in Salem. They had three children: Susannah, Margaret, and Bartholomew. Their son has the same name as William's uncle, witch trial judge Bartholomew Gedney. William was the sheriff after George Corwin, who served during the trials.

Above left: This tablet notes the graves of Francis Wainwright Sr. & Jr. It is noted as being restored in 1894. When it was restored, they put 1699 as Francis Sr.'s year of death, but records have him dying in 1692; Francis Jr. died in 1711. For Francis Jr. it once read, "Here lies entombed the body of Colonel Francis Wainwright, Esq., who died August ye 3, 1711, AEttais 47, & his vertuous consort, Mrs. Sarah, Wainwright, who died March ye 16, 1709, AEtatis 38, with three of their youngest children, John, Francis & John, who died in their infancy."

Above right: Rows of graves fill the cemetery.

Right: Mary English laid her brother and mother here to rest with a double headstone surrounded with intricate carvings. At the time they were buried here at the edge of the cemetery, the land was not filled in yet, and their graves overlooked the water.

3

Other Salem Connections: Famous Locations and Stories

While in Salem, there are a number of historical locations to visit as well as tours to take. Many of these locations and stories will have ties back to this cemetery. The graves I visited and photographed are distantly related to some of these locations, but the names stuck out to me regardless; I wanted to share a chapter on them for those that might be thinking, "Where have I heard this name before?"

First, we'll circle back to the Hathorne family. Daniel and Rachel, the grandparents of Nathaniel Hawthorne, had a daughter named Sarah on May 11, 1763. She was the fourth out of their ten children. She later married John Crowninshield, though there are no dates recording their marriage; they do not appear to have had children either. I recognized the name Crowninshield from a tour that I had taken.

The story, in short, was that Captain Joseph White was murdered in his sleep by Richard Crowninshield. He and his brother, George, had been hired by another set of brothers, the Knapps, to kill Captain White; while both Crowninshields were hired, it was confessed by Joseph Knapp that Richard was the one to kill him. The story has persisted through the years due to its violence and is even said to have inspired *The Tell-Tale Heart* by Edgar Allan Poe. Sarah's husband, John, is distantly related to Richard. John's father and Richard's grandfather were brothers.

Benjamin Felt was born in Salem sometime in 1705 to George and Jemima; he was baptized on July 22 of that year. He first married Abigail Knapp on February 16, 1728, and they had five children: Abigail (1728–1734), Benjamin, Jonathan (1737–1743), Abigail, and Jonathan (born and died 1743). After his wife's death in 1748, he married Elizabeth Ropes in November 1750. Benjamin died in 1769.

Elizabeth was born to Joseph and Hannah Ropes on July 14, 1723, as the second of eight children. I wondered if this Ropes family had any relation to the beautiful Ropes mansion. The home was built in 1727 and sold to Nathaniel Ropes in 1768. And, fun fact, the exterior was used as Allison's house in the movie *Hocus Pocus*. Elizabeth's grandfather and Nathaniel's grandfather were brothers, making them third cousins.

This photo shows the graves of Rachel Hathorne (far right), her daughter Eunice (center), and her daughter, Sarah (left). Sarah was married to John Crowninshield, second cousin of infamous murderer Richard Crowninshield. Sarah and Eunice were aunts to Nathaniel Hawthorne, author of *The Scarlet Letter*. Eunice married Aaron Porter in 1788, and they had thirteen children, though sadly lost six of them in infancy or early childhood.

These are the graves of John and Mary Crowninshield, married in 1750; they had eight children together. They too are distantly related to Richard Crowninshield. Richard's great-grandfather was brothers with John's father. There is no cause of death available for John, but Mary died in 1794 from consumption.

This is the grave of Captain Clifford Crowninshield, son of John and Mary Crowninshield. He was born in 1762 and died on June 3, 1809.

These are the graves of Benjamin and Elizabeth Felt. Elizabeth's grave (right) appears to have her name misspelled as it's shown as *Elisabeth*, though all other trees and records have her as *Elizabeth*.

This is the grave of Captain Edward Russell, born in England in 1739. There are no records of when he came to Salem, but he was married there to Abigail (Felt) Swasey on December 8, 1768. Abigail was widowed; the couple had two children, Edward and Benjamin, along with four daughters from her first marriage. Abigail was the daughter of Benjamin Felt from his first marriage.

Here you can see Edward's grave (center) and Abigail's grave (right).

4

More Stories of Salem: Other Stories from Witch City

While many are drawn to Salem due to its witch trial history, there are so many other historical stories to discover when visiting. Many can be found within the boundaries of this cemetery. Some are related to other major historical events while others give more insight into what families and day-to-day life may have been like here.

Aaron Blanchard was born on September 2, 1751; his father was also named Aaron, and his mother was Tabitha. Aaron Jr. was living in Medford in 1775 when he was twenty-four. After Paul Revere's famous ride, Aaron Jr. served in the Battle of Lexington under Isaac Hall as a minuteman. While the war was still going on, he married Anstis Dean on September 25, 1781, in Salem. Their family didn't start until after the war; their son, also named Aaron, was born on September 27, 1788. Both father and son died in 1799.

This is the grave of Revolutionary War veteran Aaron Blanchard. He died July 30, 1799; his grave has begun to sink into the earth.

This tomb was once the site of burial for Simon Bradstreet; more on his burial later. Simon was born March 18, 1603, in England to parents Simon and Margaret. He studied at Cambridge from 1621–1624 and married Anne Dudley in 1628 after having been her father's assistant. Anne is noted as being one of America's first poets and she was published in 1650.

Two years after they were married, they came to Massachusetts in 1630. From there, they started having children. They had nine in total: Ann, Samuel, Sarah, Dorothy, Simon, Hannah, Mercy, Dudley, and John. Their daughter Ann unfortunately died when she was only two years old in 1632.

The family first lived in Boston before moving all over the colony. Simon is noted for having founded Cambridge, MA. in December 1630 with Anne's father, Thomas. He also helped in the founding of Andover in 1634. He's noted as living in the following locations: Cambridge in 1634, Ipswich in 1636, Salem in 1646, Andover in 1652, Salem again in 1676, Boston in 1689, then back to Salem in 1692.

Anne died in 1652; some believe she was buried in Andover, where they were living at the time, while others think she was buried here with him. Given the time between their deaths, I think it's more likely she's buried in Andover. Simon remarried Ann Downing Gardner on May 2, 1676. She had been previously married to Joseph Gardner, who had died that year. There's no record of Ann having had children during either of her marriages; she died in 1681 and was buried here.

Simon was the governor of the colony from 1679–1686 and was the last governor to serve under Massachusetts's original charter. The charter was annulled in 1686, and he was replaced. He was governor again from 1689–1692 while a new charter was worked out. Ultimately, he was replaced by Governor Phipps under the new charter after the people of Massachusetts "lost the right" to choose their governors, instead having them assigned by the monarchy. Simon died a few years later in 1697 and was originally buried here with his second wife Ann.

Originally is the operative word. This tomb is known as a cenotaph, which is "a monument to someone buried elsewhere." While they were originally buried here, the tomb was sold to the Hathorne-Ingersoll family, and they removed the remains that were in the tomb in order to bury their own dead there. He's likely buried somewhere nearby, but there's no way to say for sure where he was buried. After what happened was discovered by researchers in the 1890s, a plaque was placed for him on his original tomb.

In one more tie back to the witch trials, Reverend Nicholas Noyes seems to have been buried here originally as well. Reverend Noyes serves as the "official minister of the trials." He presided over two of the executions, one of which was the July 19 hangings where Sarah Good died. Legend says that after she said, "You are a liar. I am no more a witch than you are a wizard," she added to Noyes, "God will give you blood to drink." Noyes died in 1717, reportedly from a hemorrhage.

Part of the plaque here reads, "He was a man endowed with keen judgement whom neither threats nor honors could sway. He weighed the authority of the king and the liberty of the people in even scales. In religion devout and upright in his ways, he vanquished the world and relinquished it on the XXVIIth (27th) day of March in the year of or Lord MDCXCVII (1697) and in the IXth (9th) year of King William Third and of his life the XCIVth (94th)."

Another of Salem's notable residents is Samuel McIntire. Born on January 16, 1757, he is described as "a prominent architect during the post-Revolutionary era in Salem." In 1981, Salem established the McIntire District, which includes both Chestnut Street and Federal Street. He was responsible for building over 400 properties, and two of his buildings are open for public visitation: the Peirce-Nichols House and Hamilton Hall. His other building credits include the Salem Courthouse (1785–1839) and South Church.

In his personal life, he married Elizabeth Field on October 10, 1778. They had a son, Samuel, who died in infancy in 1779. They had another son, also named Samuel, in 1780. He died in 1819 from intemperance when he was thirty-nine. Samuel Sr. died on February 6, 1811, when he was fifty-four.

Above left: Here is the bottom portion of Samuel McIntyre's epitaph: "He was distinguished for Genius in Architecture, Sculpture, and Musick: Modest and sweet Manners rendered him pleasing: Industry, and Integrity respectable: He professed the Religion of Jesus in his entrance on manly life; and proved its excellence by virtuous Principle and unblemished conduct."

Above right: This is the grave of Samuel's wife, Elizabeth. She was born to parents Samuel and Priscilla Field sometime around 1753.

Right: Hannah McIntire, born Hannah Hammond in 1780, was the daughter-in-law of Samuel and Elizabeth. She and their son, Samuel Jr., were married in 1804. They would have five children: Sarah, Samuel, Priscilla, Hannah, and Mary. Sadly, Samuel Jr. never got to meet his daughter Mary as she was born in 1820, and he died in September of 1819. Hannah died in 1862 from "old age."

It is no secret that medicine from the eighteenth and nineteenth centuries greatly differs from what we have available to us today. Disease ran rampant, making it a part of their everyday worries. And because things happened so quickly, many would die intestate (without a will).

William Appleton was born around 1765; he was the oldest child and only son of William and Sarah. He first married Anna Bowditch on December 22, 1793, and they had a son, William, in 1795. Both Anna and their son would pass away in 1795, on June 4 and September 1 respectively. William later remarried on July 23, 1797, to Tamesin Abbott; there are no records indicating that they had children. William was a cabinet maker with a shop at the corner of Liberty and Charter Street at that time; today, it's where the Peabody Essex museum sits, which is near the cemetery. William died in 1822 and Tamesin doesn't appear to have remarried. She was born on January 14, 1769, to George and Hannah Abbott; she died from "paralysis" in 1850.

William's first wife, Anna, was the younger sister of Ebenezer Bowditch. He was the seventh of their parents' nine children. Per probate records, Ebenezer was a goldsmith by trade. He died intestate on July 23, 1830; his son, William, was named administrator on August 17 of that year, likely because he was the only son. His older brother, also named William, lived from 1805–1806. His oldest brother, named for their father Ebenezer, died in 1825 in an almshouse.

Born in 1665 to Samuel and Martha Robinson, Samuel Robinson Jr. died intestate on October 8, 1699. On his epitaph it looks like it was spelled "Robins," and they added an "on" just above it.

Robert Stone was born sometime in either 1687 or 1688 as sources vary; Elizabeth Hardy was born around 1687 as well. They were married on Christmas Day in 1712, and they had five children: Robert Jr., Benjamin, Elizabeth, Hannah and Samuel. Robert Sr. died intestate on May 20, 1764

Samuel Phippen was born in 1744 to David and Priscilla; David was a deacon. Samuel went on to become a cabinet maker and a Windsor chair maker. He married Mary Swain on October 27, 1782, and they had two children: Rebecca and Samuel Jr. His grave says he died in 1797, but some records have it as 1798; either way, he died intestate.

This is Samuel's nephew, David Phippen. He was born July 25, 1775, to Ebenezer and Elizabeth as the second of four children. He married Nancy Cook on February 17, 1799, and they had three children of their own. He was a rope maker by trade, and he died January 14, 1849.

This is the footstone of Captain Thomas Elkins. He was born in August of 1737 and named after his father. He married Elizabeth White on November 7, 1758, and had two daughters: Martha, named after his mother, and Elizabeth. He died intestate on March 17, 1764.

Thomas Dean was a mariner and merchant, born in 1698. He married Martha Gillingham on September 18, 1720, and they had two children. Martha died on Christmas Eve in 1729. He remarried Mary Ward in November 1731, and they had one son together. Thomas died August 24, 1759, intestate like many others.

This broken grave belongs to Steven Daniel, spelled in most records as Stephen; he was the grandfather of Thomas Dean. He was born in 1632 and married Mary Prince in 1666. They had four children: twins John and Stephen, Mary and Sarah. John died in 1675 when he was six and his wife died in 1679. He later remarried Susanna Baxter, and they had a daughter. Stephen died February 14, 1686; his daughter, also named Susanna, wasn't born until August that year.

Benjamin Herbert (left) and Elizabeth (Fowler) Herbert (right) were married on January 17, 1735. Benjamin's grave spells their last name *Herbeart* and Elizabeth's grave spells her name with an S. They had eight children while they were married. Benjamin died intestate on January 20, 1761; Elizabeth remarried widower John Gardner on January 3, 1765. Even though she remarried, she is buried with her first husband.

This grave belongs to William and Tamesin Appleton. When William died in 1822, he died intestate. An appraisal of his estate was valued at $6,670 (about $180,000 today) with $115 in furniture ($3,100 today).

This is the grave of Captain Ebenezer Bowditch, brother-in-law to William Appleton twice over. William's first wife, Anna, was Ebenezer's younger sister. Ebenezer also married William's younger sister, Mary.

This is the grave of Mary Bowditch, born Mary Appleton on July 5, 1772, as the second youngest of six children. Sadly, her younger sister didn't survive infancy. She married Ebenezer Bowditch in Boston on July 25, 1797. She died on May 17, 1819.

Here you can see the graves of Captain Ebenezer Bowditch (right), his wife Mary (left), and her brother, William Appleton, behind Ebenezer.

This is the grave of Ebenezer and Mary's oldest son, Ebenezer Jr. He died by suicide on August 22, 1825, in an almshouse (also known as a poorhouse). He was only twenty-five years old.

Paralysis was a common cause of death. So common, in fact, that two of the Glover family members died from it. Ichabod Glover was born March 13, 1747, to parents Benjamin and Susanna. He was the second youngest of eleven children, with his younger sister being named Priscilla. Priscilla was born in 1750 but died in 1791 from "paraplegia." Ichabod married his wife, Mary, around 1771; when she died in 1825 at age eighty-six her cause of death is listed as "paralysis." Ichabod's cause of death is listed as being "hectic" which is likely short for "hectic fever," simply meaning it was a fever that kept coming back that they couldn't break.

Shown here are the graves of the Glover family: Priscilla (left), Mary, Mary & Susannah (center) and John (right). Priscilla and John were the siblings of Ichabod. The grave with three names in the center is for Ichabod and Mary's children. Their first daughter Mary was born February 23, 1772, but died just before her fourth birthday on February 4, 1776. Susanna, born in 1773, would die just five days after Mary on February 9, 1776. Their second daughter Mary was born in June 1777 but died September 18, 1784. No cause of death is available for the girls or their Uncle John.

Lydia Dean was born Lydia Waters sometime in 1764. There are no records to indicate when, but she married Captain Thomas Dean at some point before 1788. They had a daughter, also named Lydia, who died on July 23, 1790, when she was only two from atrophia infantilis, which is a difficulty to thrive. Lydia herself died from "fever" on January 28, 1812.

Sadly, the Deans weren't the only ones to lose young children. Joseph Hunt was born to Lewis and Mary on June 28, 1789. He was the fifth of their nine children. He had three older siblings die, one of which was before he was even born. His older sister, named Mary for their mother, died in 1785 when she was one and a half from cholera. His older brother Samuel died in 1790 just before Joseph's first birthday when he himself was almost two; his cause of death was pneumonia. When Joseph was eleven, his older brother Lewis died at age seventeen in what was listed as an "accident."

The Hodges family knew similar heartache. Gamaliel Hodges was born October 13, 1716, and married his wife Priscilla Webb on October 9, 1740. He was a merchant by trade and when he died, he left his sons 133£ each, which would be about $2,900 today. He made Priscilla the sole executor of his will and left everything else to her.

During their marriage, Gamaliel and Priscilla would have ten children: Sarah, Gamaliel, George, Benjamin, Priscilla, Gamaliel, Mary, Joseph, Benjamin, and Jonathan. Priscilla lived until 1807, outliving six of their ten children. Their first son Gamaliel lived from 1743–1752 and their first son Benjamin lived 1747–1751. Their second Gamaliel lived 1754–1768 and their second Benjamin lived 1759–1760. George died in 1764 when he was seventeen; and while Mary lived to adulthood, she died in 1791 when she was thirty-six.

Their son Joseph was born on May 7, 1758, as the eighth of their ten children. He was married in 1783 to Mary Andrew, and they had five children of their own: Mary, Gamaliel, Joseph, Priscilla and Sarah. Gamaliel and Joseph were twins. The twins were born in 1787, but Joseph would die later that year. Sarah died on September 11, 1798, when she was only eight from "fever"; she died just five days after her mother, who also died from fever.

Matthew Vincent was born December 12, 1764, and Sarah Andrews was born on June 26, 1770. They would marry on October 24, 1790, and have six children: Matthew, Nathaniel, Joseph, Elizabeth, Jonathan, and Sarah. There wasn't as much information about Jonathan and Sarah available, including birthdates, making me believe they were stillborn.

Sarah died on January 9, 1811, from dropsy, known more commonly today as edema (swelling from excess fluid in the body). When she died, her surviving children were ages thirteen to sixteen. Their father would die ten years later in Boston from intemperance, known today as excessive drinking.

George Heussler was married twice, first to Abigail Young and then to Elizabeth Lunt. He married Abigail on July 8, 1784, and they had three children: George, Margaret, and Elizabeth. Abigail died on April 21, 1799, when she was forty-six. That December, George remarried Elizabeth, and they had two children: Jane and Abigail. George and Abigail's youngest daughter, Elizabeth, died on November 1, 1823, from what's noted as phthisis pulmonalis.

"In memory of Mrs. Lydia Dean, widow of Capt. Thomas Dean, who died Jan. 28, 1819 AEt. 48"

While Joseph Hunt lost many of his siblings young, his father would also pass away when Joseph was only eight. His mother does not appear to have remarried, raising seven children on her own.

This is the grave of Sarah Hunt. Her older brother was Lewis Hunt, making her the paternal aunt of Joseph. She never married or had children. She died October 6, 1811, when she was sixty-four.

After his death in 1768, Gamaliel (spelled Gamaliell on the stone) Hodges left everything to his wife Priscilla "for her natural life." This is a bit unusual because, at that time, a lot of men would leave their estate to their wives until they got remarried, in which case everything would then pass to their sons.

This photo shows Priscilla (right) buried next to one of her and Gamaliel's sons, George, who died when he was only seventeen. It's begun to sink, but George's headstone reads, "In memory of George Hodges, son of Mr. Gamaliel Hodges Jr & Priscilla Hodges, aged 17 years. Died March ye 25th 1764."

This is the grave of Ruth Webb, born as Ruth Putnam on June 27, 1768. Her mother was Sarah Hodges, making Ruth the granddaughter of Gamaliel and Priscilla Hodges. She married Michael Webb on March 2, 1789. Their marriage would be short lived though as Ruth died on June 24, 1790, from consumption.

Joseph Hodges was the son of Gamaliel and Priscilla. He married Mary Andrew in 1783, and they had five children. After his first wife's death in 1798, he remarried Elizabeth Chipman in 1819. They had a daughter, Sarah Ellen, in 1823. Joseph died on October 7, 1826.

This is the grave of Jonathan Andrew, brother of Mary, the first wife of Joseph Hodges. Jonathan was a trader that lived at 71 Essex Street. He never married or had children, leaving everything to his nieces and nephews. He died from "lung fever" on April 18, 1844, when he was seventy-one.

Many lost their children to fever. Hannah (left) and Mary (right) were the daughters of Captain Joseph and Hannah Hosmer. Hannah was born on February 5, 1793, and Mary was born the following year in August. Hannah died on November 26, 1795, from "fever and throat," which makes me think she may have had strep. Mary followed from the same illness on December 1, just five days later.

Sarah Vincent died of dropsy in 1811, commonly referred to as edema today. This leads to swelling and oftentimes shortness of breath. Causes range from heart failure, liver disease, and kidney disease. She was forty years old when she died.

Matthew Vincent did not remarry after Sarah's death, dying himself from intemperance in 1821 when he was fifty-seven.

This is the grave of Abigail Heussler, first wife of George Heussler. She was born in 1753.

This is the grave of Elizabeth Heussler, second wife of George Heussler. She was born on March 2, 1761, and family trees show that she may have gone by "Jenny." She died March 10, 1821. Her epitaph notes her as being George's "relict" which was a term at that time for "widow."

Another woman from George's life, this is the grave of his daughter Elizabeth from his first marriage. She died when she was thirty-five from phthisis pulmonalis, which is another way of saying "consumption."

This row of graves shows some of the Heussler family graves, among others.

Susannah Babbidge died on June 3, 1804, from "fever," though her cause of death could have easily been old age as she was ninety years old when she died. A noted schoolmistress in Salem, she was born Susannah Becket in 1714. She married John Babbidge on January 11, 1732, and they had seven children. After his death in 1745, she never remarried.

Roger Peele and Margaret Bartoll were born in 1676 and 1682 respectively. While Margaret was born in Massachusetts, Roger was born in London. They married in 1709 after the death of Margaret's first husband, Thomas Kempton. Margaret already had a child from her first marriage, a son named Thomas after his father. Margaret and Roger would have three more children: Robert, Roger, and Samuel.

Their son Robert was a tailor, and he married Mary Bartlett on July 3, 1735. They had ten children: Robert, William, Ann, Mary, Margaret, Abigail, Josiah, Ann, Elizabeth, and Lydia. William was born in 1738 and was a cooper by trade, which is someone that makes wooden casks, barrels, etc. He died on March 4, 1817, from what's listed as "inflammation and rupture."

William Cook, another tailor, was born in Cambridge in 1752. I didn't see records for his first marriage, but he did have a daughter Catherine in 1777. His death records note his second wife as being Rebecca Rankin; they married November 7, 1784. William died September 27, 1803, from apoplexy, which is a brain hemorrhage/stroke. Rebecca never remarried after his death, dying May 11, 1824.

These are the graves of mother Susannah Babbidge (left) and daughter Lydia Babbidge (right). Both are noted as dying from "fever" in 1804 and 1800 respectively. Lydia, however, is noted to have been sick for ten days and her cause of death is listed as "fever and mortification." She was also the "last" of Susannah's children as she had outlived all her siblings.

Here you can see Susannah and Lydia's footstones along with their headstones.

This headstone belongs to Roger and Margaret Peele. Her name is misspelled as "Margret."

The son of Roger and Margaret, Robert married Mary Bartlett on July 3, 1735. She was born on May 10, 1713, and her parents were named Josiah and Obedience.

At the center of this photo are the footstones for Robert and Mary Peele, who died in 1773 and 1771. Buried to the left is their son, William. To the right is Josiah Peele, their grandson. He was born in 1764 to their son Robert Jr. and his wife, Elizabeth. He was only twenty years old when he died.

Margaret Hillard was the daughter of Robert and Mary Peele, born in 1742. She married Joseph Hilliard in 1763 and there is no record of them having children.

Nature has begun to grow around some of the Peele family graves.

Another cooper in Salem, Nathaniel Archer (left) was born April 17, 1710. He married Hannah Cook (right), who was born in 1713, in 1733. She died in 1767, and he died in 1772.

This is the grave of Jonathan Archer, father of Nathaniel. He was born in 1670 and died July 16, 1746.

These are the graves of William (left) and Rebecca (right) Cook. Rebecca was born in 1747 as Rebecca Rankin. Not much else is known about her outside of her marriage to William.

These graves are for Joseph and Mary Wigings. Joseph was another victim of apoplexy, dying in 1821 at age seventy-seven.

Moses Little was the town doctor after graduating from Harvard. After school, he first moved to Virginia but preferred the climate of New England and moved back. He married Elizabeth Williams on April 17, 1799, and they had three children: Elizabeth, Henry, and Francis. The family lived at 131 Essex Street. Even though Moses was a doctor, it didn't spare their family from medical disaster. Elizabeth died from consumption, also known as tuberculosis or the "white plague," on May 29, 1808. It was called "consumption" because of how the person that was infected would appear to waste away or be consumed by the disease. Their daughter, Elizabeth, died on May 2, 1810; no cause of death is given, but given how contagious tuberculosis is, it seems likely that's what caused her to die so young. Moses would die from consumption on October 13, 1811, leaving sons Henry (9) and Francis (6) orphaned.

Interesting fact about Doctor Moses Little: while he was at Harvard, he was friends with John Quincy Adams, the sixth president of the United States.

It looks like someone has previously graffitied the grave of Elizabeth Little. If this is your intent when walking into a cemetery, turn around and walk back out.

Another victim of consumption, Jonathan Peele died January 1, 1782, when he was eighty years old.

In this era, it wasn't uncommon to lose your parents when you were young or even worse, to outlive your own children.

William Wyatt was born on June 10, 1727, to parents Stephen and Mary as the second of six children. His mother died in 1737 when he was only ten; his youngest sibling was only a year old. His father would remarry Sarah Woodman in 1738, but the stability of having a mother figure would be short lived as Sarah would die in 1739; William was only twelve. His father didn't remarry again until 1759.

Captain William Wyatt married Sarah Cheever on December 30, 1756. They don't appear to have had any children.

Alice Orne and her husband, Josiah, married May 13, 1767. They had three children together: Josiah, Alice, and Susanna. Alice died on November 16, 1776, when she was only twenty-nine. Her children were eight, seven, and five. Her epitaph reads, "This stone has something great to teach, and what you need to learn, for graves my friends most loudly preach, man's infinite concern."

This is the footstone of Captain Josiah Orne, whose headstone is broken. He was first married to Alice, then after her death in 1776 he remarried Nancy White in 1778. They had seven children, but one died at age eighteen months, one was stillborn, and one died before their second birthday. Josiah himself died in 1789 when his youngest daughter was only nine months old.

This angle shows the S-shaped path winding through the headstones.

This row of headstones stands out against the red building behind the cemetery. To the right you can also see a mural peeking through.

Due to the cemetery's age, some headstones are broken or are even beginning to sink further into the earth. In this case of someone named Sarah, it appears both have occurred.

Here you can see the footstone for Robert Brookhouse, but his headstone is no longer intact.

Here you can see where some of the headstones are broken or starting to slant with age.

While some lost their parents too young, others lost their spouse. Priscilla Hodges, daughter of the previously shared Joseph Hodges, was born in 1788. She married John Jayne in 1809 when she was twenty-one. She died less than a year later on July 18, 1810.

This is the grave of Priscilla Jayne, daughter of Joseph Hodges and granddaughter of Gamaliel. Her epitaph notes her as being "the affectionate consort" of John Jayne.

"Here lyes buried the body of Mrs. Mary Masury wife to Mr. William Masury, died May 17, 1748 in the 27th year of her age"

"In memory of Mary Reed, wife of Daniel Reed Junr., who died Sept 29th 1796, aged 20 years & 6 months. Friends nor physicians could not save, my mortal body from the grave, nor can the grave confine me here, when Christ the son of God appears."

"Here lies buried the body of Mrs. Hannah Williams, the wife of Captn George Williams, who departed this life October ye 30th 1756, aged 26 years."

This is the grave of Captain George Williams, husband of Hannah. He died in 1797 when he was sixty-six.

This photo is of the cemetery from outside the fence.

Here is a view from a similar spot, this time at night.

The saddest stories of all are the ones of little ones that are gone too soon.

This is the grave of Joseph McIntire. He was born in 1785 and died in April of 1788.

This grave is too close to a post to read in its entirety. But this portion reads "Also Joseph Hillard Adams, son of Mr. John Adams, who died June 21st 1785 : Aged 1 year"

"John Herbert Tucker, son of Capt. John & Sally Tucker, died Nov. 26, 1795 aged 3 mo & 9 days"

This headstone is for John Cabot and his son, William. John, a physician, never met his son as he died on June 3, 1749; William wasn't born until October 6 of that year. William would die the following year on December 10, 1750.

Hephzibah Packer (or Packard) was born to the Drake family in Connecticut on August 21, 1658. She married Colonel Thomas Packard on August 23, 1681. They had two daughters, both named Susanna. The first lived from 1682–1683 and the second was born in 1684. Hephzibah didn't get much time with her newborn as she died on January 22, 1684, when she was only twenty-five.

While not a little one, Moses Lawrence was still too young when he passed away. He was born in 1807 and died October 7, 1826, when he was only nineteen. His epitaph lists his parents as Schuyler and Lucy.

"Here lyes ye body of Edward Dean, son of Mr. Philemon Dean of Ipswich, who died Sept 14, 1716, aged 21 years."

"In memory of Stephen Smith who died April 3, 1815 in the 20 year of his age. Thoughtless wanderer, turn aside. And read when Stephen Smith died. You too must die and lay your head in this cold lodging of the dead. If you are young, so too was I. If you are old, you soon must die. Then listen to the solemn word ... " and the rest is cut off.

Nabby Frye was born on April 5, 1795, to parents Peter and Abigail. Nabby was her mother's nickname and it's not clear if she was named Nabby or had the same nickname as her mother for Abigail. She was the younger of two sisters, with Polly being born in 1792. Nabby died on June 30, 1800, when she was five; Polly died when she was eleven on April 5, 1803.

This is the grave of Nabby's mother, also called Nabby. Her mother died in 1802, two years after her and a year before her oldest daughter, Polly. She was only thirty-eight when she died. In three years, Peter Frye lost his wife and both of his daughters. He never remarried and lived until 1815, dying from consumption.

Sarah Fitz was born in 1773, though most records note her as going by Sally. She married Jonathan Ashby on November 11, 1792. They had a daughter, also named Sally, on March 13, 1793. Sally died when she was three years old in October 1796. They had six more children: Jonathan, Benjamin, William, John, Sally, and Elizabeth. Their first son Jonathan died shortly after he was born in 1794. William and John both died in 1805 at ages six and four.

This is the grave of Sally Ashby, who suffered many losses as a mother. Out of her seven children, one died in infancy and three died in early childhood.

This is the grave of Jonathan Ashby, the father-in-law of Sally. He was born on July 21, 1746, and died on November 15, 1797.

This is the grave of Mary Ashby, though she went by Polly. She was the sister-in-law of Jonathan Ashby, making her the great-aunt of Sally's children. She was born in the Field family in 1758 and died April 3, 1789.

This photo overlooks the section where the Ashbys are buried.

Charter Street Cemetery is the oldest in Salem, established in 1637.

Because it's the oldest cemetery in Salem, it is also one of the oldest cemeteries in the United States.

I could (and have) spent hours wandering this cemetery's paths.

References

Family tree sources provided by findagrave.com, ancestry.com, Family Tree app and Geneanet community trees index.

American Marriages Before 1699 [database on-line]. Provo, UT, USA: Ancestry.com Operations Inc, 1997.

Austin, Joel. "The Salem Witch Trials Memorial: History, Tours, & More!" *ToSalem*, 1 June 2024, tosalem.com/salem-witch-trials-memorial/.

Baltrusis, S. (2019). *Wicked salem: Exploring lingering lore and legends.* Globe Pequot, An imprint of The Rowman & Littlefield Publishing Group, Inc.

Barton, Mariana, and Elva Gerlach. "The True Story of Bathsheba Sherman – the Ghost from 'The Conjuring.'" *History Mystery*, 26 Oct. 2023, historymystery.net/the-true-story-of-bathsheba-sherman-the-ghost-from-the-conjuring/.

"Battles of Lexington and Concord - Winner, Date, Summary." *History.Com*, A&E Television Networks, 27 Feb. 2025, www.history.com/topics/american-revolution/battles-of-lexington-and-concord.

Biographies of Notable Americans, 1904 [database on-line]. Provo, UT, USA: Ancestry.com Operations Inc, 1997.

"Bold Hawthorne." *Collection at Bartleby.Com*, 22 Nov. 2022, www.bartleby.com/lit-hub/a-library-of-american-literature/bold-hawthorne/.

Boston, Massachusetts, US, Marriages, 1700-1809

Brooks, Rebecca Beatrice, et al. "Salem Witch Trials Memorial." *History of Massachusetts Blog*, 14 Feb. 2025, historyofmassachusetts.org/salem-witch-trials-memorial/.

Brooks, Rebecca Beatrice, Bethany Downey, et al. "The Witchcraft Trial of Samuel Wardwell." *History of Massachusetts Blog*, 3 Oct. 2021, historyofmassachusetts.org/samuel-wardwell-salem/.

Brooks, Rebecca Beatrice, Jean Genasci, et al. "The Witchcraft Trial of Margaret Scott." *History of Massachusetts Blog*, 7 July 2023, historyofmassachusetts.org/margaret-scott-salem/.

Brooks, Rebecca Beatrice, Kathie Johnson, et al. "The Witchcraft Trial of Mary Parker." *History of Massachusetts Blog*, 7 July 2023, historyofmassachusetts.org/mary-parker-salem/.

Brooks, Rebecca Beatrice, Kenneth Reitman, et al. "The Witchcraft Trial of Martha Corey." *History of Massachusetts Blog*, 24 Jan. 2025, historyofmassachusetts.org/martha-corey/.

Brooks, Rebecca Beatrice, Mary Casto, et al. "The Witchcraft Trial of Ann Pudeator." *History of Massachusetts Blog*, 7 July 2023, historyofmassachusetts.org/ann-pudeator-salem/.

Brooks, R. B., & Cohen, N. V. (2022, August 21). The witchcraft trial of Philip English. *History of Massachusetts Blog*. https://historyofmassachusetts.org/philip-english-salem/

Brooks, R. B., Crean-Carter , W., Switlik, J., Callahan, J., Turner, J., Hibbard, L., Musgrave, B., & Dyer, D. (2021, October 24). John Hathorne: Salem witch judge. *History of Massachusetts Blog*. https://historyofmassachusetts.org/john-hathorne-the-salem-witch-judge/

Brooks, R. B., Engel May, E. (Liz), & Calabrese, C. (2022, May 23). History of the Ropes Mansion in Salem, Massachusetts. *History of Massachusetts Blog.* https://historyofmassachusetts.org/ropes-mansion-salem/

Captain John Putnam Home, site of. Salem Witch Museum. (2020, January 2). https://salemwitchmuseum.com/locations/captain-john-putnam-home-site-of/

"Charter Street Cemetery: Salem Ma Witch Trial Historical Locations." *Salem Witch Museum*, 12 Feb. 2024, salemwitchmuseum.com/locations/old-burying-point-charter-street-cemetery/.

Cherry, Kendra. "What Is Catalepsy?" *Verywell Mind*, Verywell Mind, 21 Dec. 2021, www.verywellmind.com/catalepsy-signs-causes-treatment-and-coping-5212828.

"Chronology." *Salem, Massachusetts - Your Guide to the Witch City*, 23 Mar. 2022, salemweb.com/witches/the-salem-witch-trials/chronology/.

Danvers, Essex County, Massachusetts Births to 1850

Data concerning the families of Bancroft, Bradstreet, Browne, Dudley, Emerson, Gamble, Goodridge, Gould, Hartshorne, Hobson, Kemp, Kendall, Metcalf, Nichols, Parker, Poole, Sawtell, Wainwright, Woodman, etc. in England and America, 1277 to 1906 A.D. [database on-line]. Provo, UT: Ancestry.com Operations Inc, 2005.

DeLong, William. "The Story of Giles Corey, the 80-Year-Old Salem Farmer Slowly Crushed to Death for Witchcraft." *All That's Interesting*, 8 Oct. 2021, allthatsinteresting.com/giles-corey-martha-corey.

Essex Institute Historical Collections. (1903). (Vol. 39). Essex Institute Press.

Essex, Massachusetts Probate Records, 1648–1840

Family tree of Samuel Sewall - Geneastar. (n.d.). https://en.geneastar.org/genealogy/sewallsamue/samuel-sewall

"Hobbs Family Home, Site Of." *Salem Witch Museum*, 11 June 2024, salemwitchmuseum.com/locations/hobbs-family-home-site-of/.

"Ingersoll's Ordinary." *Salem Witch Museum*, 14 Feb. 2019, salemwitchmuseum.com/locations/ingersolls-ordinary/.

Katz, Brigit. "Last Convicted Salem 'witch' Is Finally Cleared." *Smithsonian.Com*, Smithsonian Institution, 3 Aug. 2022, www.smithsonianmag.com/smart-news/last-convicted-salem-witch-is-finally-cleared-180980516/.

Landrigan, Leslie. "A Sad Condition: Wilmot Redd and the Salem Witch Trials." *New England Historical Society*, 7 Oct. 2024, newenglandhistoricalsociety.com/sad-condition-wilmot-redd-salem-witch-trials/.

Mackenzie, G. N. (1909). *Colonial families of the United States of America.* Genealogical Publishing Co.

Massachusetts Deaths, 1844: Vol. 8, Barnstable to Hampshire; Volume 9, Middlesex to Worcester

Massachusetts, US, Compiled Birth, Marriage and Death Records, 1700–1850

Massachusetts, US, Compiled Marriage Records, 1633–1850

Massachusetts, US, Death Records, 1841–1915

Massachusetts, US, Marriage Index, 1784–1840

Massachusetts, US, Marriage Records, 1840–1915

Massachusetts, US, Soldiers and Sailors in the Revolutionary War, Vol. 6

Massachusetts, US, Town and Vital Records, 1620–1988

Massachusetts, US, Town Birth Records, 1620–1850

Massachusetts, US, Vital Records, 1640–1849

Massachusetts, US, Wills and Probate Records, 1635–1991

"Massachusetts Clears 5 from Salem Witch Trials." *The New York Times*, 2 Nov. 2001, www.nytimes.com/2001/11/02/us/massachusetts-clears-5-from-salem-witch-trials.html.

"McIntire District." *Preserving Salem*, www.preservingsalem.com/mcintire-district. Accessed 3 Apr. 2025.

"Medford Early History – 17th and 18th Centuries." *Medford Historical Society & Museum*, 26 Apr. 2021, medfordhistorical.org/mapping-medford/walking-tours/medford-early-history/.
"Minute Man Soldier Search - *Friends of Minute Man National Park*." Friends of Minute Man National Park -, 26 Nov. 2024, friendsofminuteman.org/soldier-search/.
"Nathaniel Hawthorne Birthplace, Salem, Mass." *Lost New England*, 23 Dec. 2023, lostnewengland.com/2019/01/nathaniel-hawthorne-birthplace-salem-mass/.
New England Historical & Genealogical Register, 1847–2011
New England, *The Great Migration and The Great Migration Begins*, 1620-1635 [database on-line]. Provo, UT, USA: Ancestry.com Operations, Inc., 2013.
North America, Family Histories, 1500–2000
Older rationales and other challenges in handling causes of death in historical individual-level databases: the case of Copenhagen, 1880–1881
Barbara Revuelta-Eugercios, Helene Castenbrandt, Anne Løkke Author Notes
"The Pardoning of Ann Pudeator." *Streetsofsalem*, 22 Sept. 2015, streetsofsalem.com/2015/09/22/the-pardoning-of-ann-pudeator/.
Reverend John Higginson Home, site of / salem witch museum. Salem Witch Museum. (2021, March 4). https://salemwitchmuseum.com/locations/reverend-john-higginson-home-site-of-salem-witch-museum/
Roach, M. K. (2020). *Six women of salem: The untold story of the accused and their accusers in the Salem Witch Trials*. Hachette Books.
"Sarah Good - the Tragic Story of a Poor Woman Accused of Witchcraft." *1692 Before And After - Historical Walking Tour in Salem, MA*, 13 Mar. 2025, 1692beforeandafter.com/sarah-good-the-tragic-story-of-a-poor-woman-accused-of-witchcraft/.
Schiff, S. (2015). *The Witches: Salem, 1692*. Little, Brown and Company.
Snyder, Heather. "Giles Corey." Salem Witch Trials: Giles Corey, salem.lib.virginia.edu/people/gilescorey.html. Accessed 3 Apr. 2025.
Social History of Medicine, Volume 35, Issue 4, November 2022, Pages 1116–1139, https://doi.org/10.1093/shm/hkab037 Published: 08 October 2021
"SWP No. 045: Mary Esty Executed, September 22, 1692." *SWP No. 045: Mary Esty Executed, September 22, 1692 - New Salem - Pelican*, salem.lib.virginia.edu/n45.html#n45.22. Accessed 3 Apr. 2025.
"SWP No. 173: Reversal of Attainder and Restitution (1710 - 1750)." *SWP No. 173: Reversal of Attainder and Restitution (1710 - 1750)* - New Salem - Pelican, salem.lib.virginia.edu/n173.html#n173.47. Accessed 3 Apr. 2025.
"SWP No. 173: Reversal of Attainder and Restitution (1710 - 1750)." SWP No. 173: *Reversal of Attainder and Restitution (1710 - 1750)* - New Salem - Pelican, salem.lib.virginia.edu/n173.html. Accessed 3 Apr. 2025.
"The Salem Witchcraft Papers." *Swp - New Salem - Pelican*, salem.lib.virginia.edu/category/swp.html. Accessed 3 Apr. 2025.
"Strong Women of the Gables: Susanna Ingersoll." *The House of the Seven Gables*, 14 Feb. 2023, 7gables.org/2018/02/28/strong-women-gables/.
Thornber, Craig. "Glossary of Medical Terms Used in the 18th and 19th Centuries." *Glossary of Old Medical Terms*, www.thornber.net/medicine/html/medgloss.html. Accessed 3 Apr. 2025.
US, New England Marriages Prior to 1700
US, Newspaper Extractions from the Northeast, 1704–1930
Wagner, E. (2010). A murder in Salem | smithsonian. *Smithsonian Magazine*. https://www.smithsonianmag.com/history/a-murder-in-salem-64885035/
"Wilmot Redd, the Witch of Marblehead." NEW ENGLAND FOLKLORE, newenglandfolklore.blogspot.com/2022/04/wilmot-redd-witch-of-marblehead.html. Accessed 3 Apr. 2025.
"Witch Trials Memorial." *Salem Witch Museum*, 27 Feb. 2025, salemwitchmuseum.com/locations/witch-trials-memorial/.

Yost, Russell. "Elizabeth Howe Trial and Execution." *The History Junkie*, 3 Nov. 2023, thehistoryjunkie.com/elizabeth-howe-trial-and-execution/.
Yost, Russell. "John Proctor Family Tree and Descendants." *The History Junkie*, 19 Oct. 2023, thehistoryjunkie.com/john-proctor-family-tree-and-descendants/#family-tree-chart.
Yost, Russell. "Margaret Scott Facts and Salem Witch Trials." *The History Junkie*, 3 Nov. 2023, thehistoryjunkie.com/margaret-scott-facts-and-salem-witch-trials/.
Yost, Russell. "Mary Bradbury and the Salem Witch Trials." *The History Junkie*, 3 Nov. 2023, thehistoryjunkie.com/mary-bradbury-and-the-salem-witch-trials/.
Yost, Russell. "Nicholas Noyes and the Salem Witch Trials." *The History Junkie*, 1 Nov. 2023, thehistoryjunkie.com/nicholas-noyes-and-the-salem-witch-trials/.